D1263281

# T-Lloyd
# In the Trenches

## By Ron Berman and Stephen McFadden

www.av2books.com

**Your AV² Media Enhanced book gives you an online audio book, and a self-assessment activity. Log on to www.av2books.com and enter the unique book code from this page to access these special features.**

Go to **www.av2books.com**, and enter this book's unique code.

**BOOK CODE**

**Q29435**

AV² **by Weigl** brings you media enhanced books that support active learning.

# AV² Audio Chapter Book Navigation

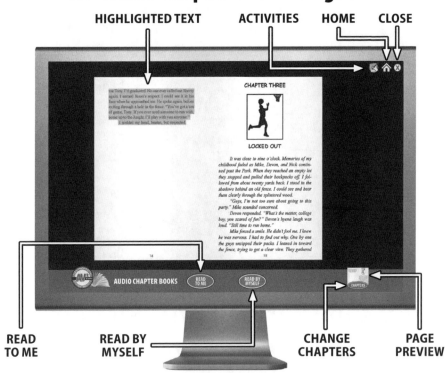

HIGHLIGHTED TEXT    ACTIVITIES    HOME    CLOSE

READ TO ME    READ BY MYSELF    CHANGE CHAPTERS    PAGE PREVIEW

Published by AV² by Weigl
350 5th Avenue, 59th Floor
New York, NY 10118

Website: www.av2books.com    www.weigl.com

First Published by Scobre Educational Press.

Library of Congress Control Number: 2013937458
ISBN 978-1-62127-991-4 (hardcover)
ISBN 978-1-62127-947-1 (single-user eBook)
ISBN 978-1-48960-022-6 (multi-user eBook)

Printed in the United States of America in North Mankato, Minnesota
1 2 3 4 5 6 7 8 9 0  17 16 15 14 13

062013
WEP310513

2

# TABLE OF CONTENTS

# CHAPTER ONE

## THE LINE

Everything is quiet on the line. Almost *too* quiet. The sounds of the crowd seem far away. The players line up across from each another in a 3-point stance. These guys are *huge*. In a few seconds, the ball will be hiked. When that happens, it won't be quiet anymore. The field will turn into a war zone.

Coaches yell advice from the sidelines, but it doesn't matter right now. The guys on the line know what to do. Each player looks right at the person he will soon be doing battle with. There are just a few inches between them.

The line between these players is called the line of scrimmage. It's where every play in a football game begins. The line can't be crossed by either team until the ball is hiked. This area is known to football players as the trenches. On both sides of the line are some of the strongest men in the world. They are the offensive and defensive linemen.

The action in the trenches is not pretty. It's brutal. Linemen are trained to hit hard, and they never show mercy. They want to strike quickly and with great power.

The stuff that happens on the line is very important. It changes almost everything else that happens in a football game. Sure, it's the quarterback who leads his team down the field. It's the running back who explodes for a first down. And it's the wide receiver who catches a pass for a touchdown. But none of that will happen if the guys on the line don't do their jobs.

Football holds a special place in the hearts of Americans. Millions of fans tune in every year. They root for their favorite teams. The Super Bowl is the biggest game of the year. It's watched by more than 130 million people from around the world.

Across the country, young football players are training hard every day. When summer ends and fall arrives, it's time for high school football. In small towns and large cities, big games take place every week. For these high school players, it's all about the love of football. For many of them, it's also about trying to earn a college scholarship.

College is a whole different level, of course. The players are bigger, faster, and stronger. Star players are thinking about making it in the pros. This is something they've been dreaming about for their whole lives. Now, it's so close they can almost taste it. They know how tough it is. Less than 300 players are drafted into the NFL every year. Still, for star college football players, that's the goal they are shooting for.

The NFL draft, held in New York City every year since 1965, is exciting for both NFL hopefuls and fans watching the action at home. Pictured above, reporters anxiously await the Chicago Bears decision on their first round pick.

Playing football is a lot of fun. The only thing that is just as exciting is watching a game in person. Most fans, when they can't go to a game, watch it on TV. But many football fans only watch *part* of the game. That's because the cameras only follow the ball. Yet there are 22 players on the field at all times. So, by only watching the ball, fans don't see everything that's happening—especially in the trenches.

**When the camera follows the ball, everyone else becomes a blur in the background.**

When a play ends, the cameras turn to the quarterback. We see his anger when he throws an interception. We also see the joy on his face when he tosses a pass for a first down. But the quarterback isn't doing it all by himself. Most people don't realize how much he depends on his teammates. The offensive line has to block the defenders to give him time to throw. If anyone doesn't do his job, the whole play breaks down.

To win a football game, an all-around team effort is needed. There are 53 players on each NFL squad. That's more than teams in other major sports. Any one of these players might play a big role in the game.

Teamwork starts in the huddle. The players gather around the quarterback, who calls a play. On the other side of the ball, the defensive line gets ready. They want to put pressure on the quarterback. They also want to create a wall of bodies that running backs can't get by. The next time you watch a football game in person, try something. For a few plays, don't follow the ball. Instead, watch the action that is taking place at the line of scrimmage.

Okay, so maybe most fans don't pay attention to what's happening in the trenches. But coaches and star football players certainly do. In 1991, Emmitt Smith of the Dallas Cowboys rushed for 1,563 yards. What did he do? He bought $5,000 Rolex watches for *each* player on his offensive line! He knew how important their blocking was. Without it, he wouldn't have had such a great season. As one coach says, "The line is the key. If you can't protect the quarterback and run the ball, the game is lost."

For every offensive player, there is a defensive player. The cornerbacks and safeties guard the receivers. The linebackers usually play between the linemen and the safeties and corners. Linebackers follow the ball. If it's a running play, they attack the line of scrimmage. There, they look to make a tackle. If it's a passing play, they have a couple of options. They either attack the quarterback or drop back to cover the pass.

Defensive linemen are different. They try to plug the holes in the line. They also try to keep the offensive lineman from pushing them backward. If they get the chance, they will go after the quarterback or running back. But that's not their main job. They are just trying to keep the other team from moving forward.

That's what defense is all about—trying to *stop* awesome players like Tony Romo or Adrian Peterson. It's not easy, of course. Any coach in the NFL will tell you that defense wins championships.

**Above is the prestigious Vince Lombardi trophy, awarded each year to the winner of the Super Bowl. The award had originally been named the "World Championship Game Trophy." It was later renamed in honor of Coach Lombardi.**

Here's a quiz: think of your favorite NFL team and name the nose tackle. No clue? Well, you're not the only one. Most football fans couldn't tell you who their nose tackle is. But he is one of the most important players on the field. The nose tackle is also sometimes called the nose guard. He lines up on the *nose* of the football, across from the center. He's right there in the heart of the trenches.

When the ball is snapped, one or two blockers crash into the nose tackle—on *every* play. He must hold his ground so his teammates can make a play. This is why many coaches consider the nose tackle to be so important. If he is getting pushed backward, the offense is probably moving down the field. But if the nose tackle is doing his job, it changes everything. In that case, a lot of offensive linemen have to worry about him. That means that there are fewer guys protecting the quarterback.

A nose tackle has to be willing to take a lot of punishment. Put on your helmet, get out there, and get *pounded* ... on every play! That's the life of a nose tackle. It's a tough position, that's for sure. Bob Golic knows all about it. He was an all-pro nose tackle. He once said, "If you're mad at your kid, you can raise him to be a nose tackle. Or, just send him out to play on the *freeway*. It's about the same."

Golic's funny statement makes a good point. Nose tackles take a lot of pounding during a football game. So why would anyone *want* to play this position? Well, one amazing young athlete knows why. His name is Thomas Lloyd III, known to his family as "T.J." With his friends, though, and on the football field, he goes by "T-Lloyd."

This 18-year-old nose tackle is from Hurst, Texas. Before that, he lived in New Orleans. He has loved the sport of football his entire life. But he wasn't born to play quarterback or wide receiver. T-Lloyd was built for the trenches. He's a team player who never gives up. At just under 270 pounds, he's an awesome force on the football field.

Vince Lombardi might have been the greatest coach in the history of football. He once said, "Individual commitment to a group effort—that is what makes a team work." He meant that doing your best *for the team* is the most important thing. Nobody understands this better than nose tackles. One of the best of them is Thomas Lloyd III—T-Lloyd.

**T-Lloyd (in the white shirt and white hat) poses with some of his teammates.**

# CHAPTER TWO

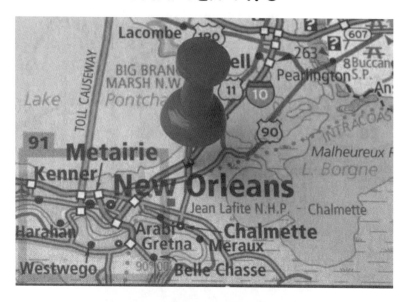

## ROUGH BEGINNING

"It's just not fair," 10-year-old Thomas said. He tried to hold back the tears. Today was tryouts for Pop Warner football. The coach had just told Thomas that he was too big to play. The weight limit was 135 pounds, but he weighed 160 pounds.

The other boys seemed happy. None of them wanted to go head-to-head with Thomas! When he left the field with his father, Thomas was really upset. He had wanted to play football ever since he could remember

Growing up in New Orleans, Thomas Lloyd III watched football every weekend. He looked forward to college football on Saturdays. Then, on Sundays, it was NFL games. He always cheered for his favorite teams, like the New Orleans Saints.

T-Lloyd also roots for the LSU Tigers.

Thomas couldn't get enough of football. His dad used to be a high school linebacker. Mr. Lloyd explained everything about the game to his son. Thomas found out about the action that takes place on the line of scrimmage. He learned how each player does his part to help the team win.

The next couple of weeks were tough on Thomas. He was still angry about being left out of Pop Warner. Then one day he passed by some older kids in the neighborhood. They were playing a pick-up football game. Thomas walked up to them and asked if he could play. Even though he was younger, he was still bigger than most of them. Thomas started playing with those kids all the time. It was the next best thing to being on a real team.

Although pick-up football was fun, it wasn't the same as Pop Warner. This youth football league has been around for a long time. It teaches football to thousands of kids every year. That was exactly what Thomas needed. He wanted to become a better player. Pick-up games didn't prepare him for team competition.

Luckily, Thomas' dad was there for him. Even though Mr. Lloyd was busy, he found time to work with his son. They practiced many things, like how to get into a three-point stance.

The lessons continued for the next few years. One night, Mr. Lloyd came into Thomas' bedroom to say goodnight. Thomas was wearing his pajamas— and a New Orleans Saints helmet! He was pretending to line up on the offensive line. It was something they had been practicing.

Looking up, Thomas smiled. "Remember how they didn't let me play on Pop Warner a couple of years ago? Well, I don't care about that anymore. I'll be ready once middle school starts. Nobody's gonna stop me from making the team."

By the time Thomas entered middle school, he weighed 220 pounds. He was huge, strong, and in good shape. All he could think about was becoming a member of the team.

It's hard going to a new school and meeting new people. Not for Thomas. He is a very friendly and outgoing guy. Making friends was easy for him.

But things were tougher on the football field. Thomas was only a sixth grader. Most of the other guys were seventh or eighth graders. They had a better chance of making the team.

It turned out to be a rough beginning for Thomas. The drills the coaches ran were totally new to him. One of them was the "2 on 1" drill. This drill is all about taking on a double team. Two players line up and block a single player. That player tries to get past them. It's a hard drill for someone who has never done it before.

Between long practices and learning new drills, Thomas had a tough time. But he never quit. The coaches saw his good attitude. They saw him getting knocked down over and over, but quickly getting up. At one point, a coach asked Thomas if he needed a break. Thomas refused. He didn't want to give up.

Thomas' hard work paid off. He made the team, which made him very happy. He hoped to get a lot of playing time. But week after week, he watched from the sidelines. The coaches were playing the other kids instead. Thomas was busting his butt in practice, but it wasn't enough.

It was late in the season when Thomas finally got his chance. His team was ahead 21-6 with only five minutes left in the game. This blow-out meant that the starters could get some rest. The coach looked over at Thomas and yelled, "Get in there, Grunt!" (Grunt is a word that means lineman.)

Thomas put on his helmet and ran onto the field. He took his spot on the defensive line. As soon as the center snapped the ball, Thomas charged forward. He crashed into two offensive linemen. He forced his way between them with a strong move. Breaking free, he tackled the quarterback. He made a sack on his first play ever!

It was an exciting moment for Thomas. Yet, looking back on it, he laughs. "I had no clue what I was doing out there. I was just so happy to be on the field. I don't know if that first play was luck or skill. But I can't think of a better way to start my football career!"

That play was only the beginning. Thomas soon earned a starting spot on the defensive line. Every week he got better and better.

By the time he graduated from middle school, Thomas Lloyd III was a different player. He even earned a nickname: "T-Lloyd." He was looking forward to high school. St. Bernard had a great football team. It was going to be tough to prove himself. Still, he knew someday he would make the varsity. Nothing was going to stop T-Lloyd from being a great high school football player.

# CHAPTER THREE

## THE STORM

When the bell rang, everyone cheered. It was the last day of class before summer vacation. T-Lloyd had a big smile on his face. It was June of 2005. His first year of high school was over.

It had been a great year for T-Lloyd. For the first time ever, he felt like a *real* football player. His hard work on the field had earned him a spot on varsity. And he was only a freshman! True, he wasn't playing nose tackle yet. That's the position that would later make him a high school star. For now, he had turned into a good offensive lineman.

Making varsity as a freshman is really tough. It was cool that T-Lloyd made it. Still, he wasn't happy with just getting a spot on the team. He wanted even more. So he tried his hardest every day at practice, and during games. It all paid off when he earned all-league honors.

That wasn't the only honor T-Lloyd earned that year. He also won the "Coach's Award." This award is given to the player who works the hardest. The honor taught T-Lloyd an important lesson. He learned that being successful in football takes a lot of dedication.

**T-Lloyd has always gotten along with his coaches.**

T-Lloyd was looking forward to summer vacation. He planned to hang out with his friends and do some weightlifting. Everything seemed perfect.

A few months later, T-Lloyd was on his way to the gym. Summer was a lot of fun so far. He was driving along and feeling good. The radio was playing

"On my Own," by Lil' Wayne. The bass shook the car as T-Lloyd rolled to the beat.

All of a sudden, T-Lloyd's cell phone beeped. Someone had sent him a text message. He stopped a few minutes later and looked down at his phone. The text message was from his mom. "Did you hear about the storm?" she asked. "Come home as soon as you can."

It was Wednesday, August 24, 2005. T-Lloyd knew what his mom was talking about. He had seen the reports that had been on TV lately. There was a huge storm headed to Florida. T-Lloyd's home in New Orleans was about 200 miles away from Florida. "Yeah, no big deal," he texted back. "I'll be home after the gym."

When T-Lloyd returned home later, the storm had grown stronger. By the next day, it was even more powerful. It was now a hurricane. It had even been given a name: *Katrina*. That was a name that everyone in America would soon hear about.

What is a hurricane? It's a powerful storm with very fast winds. The winds of a hurricane can cause a lot of damage. When a hurricane hits, the best thing to do is leave the area.

The Lloyd family talked about all of these things. At the moment, the hurricane was far away. But there was a chance it might reach New Orleans.

The Lloyds were not too worried at first. The same thing had happened a year before. A big storm was supposed to come. They left their home and returned the next day. When they came back, the house was okay. "We thought this would be the same thing," T-Lloyd says. "We thought we were going to leave and then come back soon."

It was now Friday, August 26. T-Lloyd and his younger brother Tevin got into the car with their mom. They were going to Dallas, Texas. It takes five hours to get there. Mr. Lloyd stayed behind. He was going to make sure their house was okay.

Right away Mrs. Lloyd and her sons knew something was wrong. The roads were filled with cars trying to get out of town. It took them 26 hours to get to Dallas!

Mrs. Lloyd and her boys finally made it to their aunt's home in Dallas. They quickly turned on the television. They were scared by what they saw.

Katrina destroyed nearly everything in its path.

Most of New Orleans was flooded—even their high school.

In the aftermath of Hurricane Katrina, New Orleans looked more like a river than a city.

The news was saying that Hurricane *Katrina* was one of the worst storms ever. And Mr. Lloyd was still in the middle of it! T-Lloyd tried to call him, but every call went straight to voicemail. T-Lloyd and his family started to pray. They prayed that Mr. Lloyd was safe.

The next couple of days were hard for the Lloyds. The storm was getting worse and worse. Many homes were destroyed and people were dying. T-Lloyd was very worried about his father.

By Sunday, August 28, T-Lloyd was feeling

awful. The winds from Hurricane *Katrina* were almost 200 miles per hour. To show how scary that is, check this out: a NASCAR driver can go as fast as 200 miles per hour!

The worst part for the Lloyd family was not knowing if Mr. Lloyd was safe. T-Lloyd hadn't heard from his dad in almost three days. It was very painful to see the pictures of dead bodies floating down the street. T-Lloyd prayed that his father wasn't one of them.

There was a lot going on in T-Lloyd's heart. He couldn't stop thinking about his dad and all the good times they had together. He remembered them talking, laughing, and watching football. There were just so many memories. The thought of losing his father was almost too much to take.

Two days later, T-Lloyd was feeling very sad.

He couldn't take his eyes off the TV. But watching just made things worse. It was one awful thing after another. People didn't have food or fresh water, and they were dying. Houses were destroyed. Nothing seemed to be getting better. *How can this be happening?* T-Lloyd wondered. He was losing hope.

And then the phone rang…

T-Lloyd jumped out of his chair to answer the phone. "Hello," he said. He was more nervous than he had ever been before. The last week had been the worst of his life. Was this phone call going to bring even more horrible news? *Is my dad alive or not?* That was the question on T-Lloyd's mind.

Hearing the phone ring, T-Lloyd's family had rushed into the room. Now they were looking at T-Lloyd, hoping for good news. When T-Lloyd heard his father's voice, it was the greatest feeling! He was so happy. He yelled out, "Dad! You're okay!" The whole family started screaming and hugging each other. It was a moment they would never forget.

Mr. Lloyd explained what happened. When the hurricane hit, the streets were flooded with water. It was too dangerous for Mr. Lloyd to stay in the house. He saw a car floating down the street and he jumped on. He had to hold on tightly!

That was just the beginning. From there, Mr. Lloyd made it onto the roof of a building. Other people were there, too. There was very little water to drink, and nothing to eat. They were all cold, wet, and scared.

But they didn't give up. Neither did Mr. Lloyd. He just kept thinking about his wife, T-Lloyd, and Tevin. He wanted to see them again.

A few days later, Mr. Lloyd got a ride on a boat to a shelter. Hundreds of other people were there also. He spent two more days there. Then he was moved to a better shelter. He was able to get some food for the first time in five days. More importantly, somebody let him borrow a cell phone. As soon as he heard T-Lloyd's voice, Mr. Lloyd knew it was all worth it.

A couple of days later, Mr. Lloyd flew to Dallas. The whole family met at the airport. They cried and hugged each other.

**Reunited.**

All they cared about was that Mr. Lloyd was safe. But they still had problems to face. Would the family be able to return home? Would T-Lloyd and Tevin be able to start school again in New Orleans?

T-Lloyd didn't think about that stuff at first. He was just happy to see his dad. Still, his life was about to change. He didn't know what would happen next.

**T-Lloyd ponders his future.**

# CHAPTER FOUR

## FRIDAY NIGHT LIGHTS

Once in a while, T-Lloyd pulls out the trophy and looks at it. It's a simple wooden trophy with the words "Coach's Award 2004." He earned it after his freshman season at in New Orleans.

T-Lloyd doesn't need honors or awards to get him pumped up. Still, the Coach's Award trophy is important. It is one of the few things that wasn't destroyed by the hurricane. T-Lloyd thinks about everything that has happened since then. One minute he was getting ready for his sophomore year of high school. Then Hurricane *Katrina* changed his life forever.

After the storm, the Lloyds returned to their home—or what was left of it. The key to the front door didn't even work anymore. Mr. Lloyd had to kick in the door just to get inside. There was mud and water everywhere. The walls were falling apart. The furniture was destroyed. They couldn't live in the house anymore. So Mr. and Mrs. Lloyd decided they had to move.

The Lloyds weren't the only family that was hurt by Hurricane *Katrina*. Close to 2,000 people died. Thousands of homes were damaged. The storm caused $81 *billion* worth of damage.

Like many families from New Orleans, the Lloyds needed a new place to live. Texas seemed to be a good choice because they had family there. Mr. and Mrs. Lloyd were given some help from the government. With that help, they were able to find an apartment.

T-Lloyd soon headed back to Texas. He used to come there to visit family. Now it was his new home. T-Lloyd wondered what life would be like in the "Lone Star State."

Many people like to say, "Everything is bigger in Texas." It's really true. Texas is a huge state, with 20 million people living there. Driving from one end of the state to the other would take over ten hours. Another thing that's huge in Texas is sports. It's such a big state that it has two NFL teams, two Major League baseball teams, and *three* NBA teams.

Leaving New Orleans was sad for T-Lloyd. Still, he was excited about moving to Texas. People in Texas love high school football. They are very proud of their teams. It's normal to have as many as 10,000 fans watch a game!

There is even a book about Texas high school football. It's called "Friday Night Lights." The book was turned into a movie and a hit TV show. It's about a small town and its love of high school football. The book makes a good point: In Texas, football is more than a sport ... it's almost like a religion.

T-Lloyd knew all this. He would miss his friends back home, but this was a great chance for him. Texas is an important football state. More NFL players come from Texas than any other state. It's very simple—if you're good in Texas, *everybody* knows about it. There are newspapers, magazines, and TV shows. Plus there are many college scouts.

The Lloyds moved to a small city called Hurst. Of course, it's never easy to start over at a new school. Still, T-Lloyd and Tevin had a good attitude about it. Soon T-Lloyd was walking around Hurst L.D. Bell High School. He couldn't believe his eyes. The weight room, stadium, and even the locker room were all huge!

T-Lloyd got used to his new home very quickly. Making friends was no problem. He became popular almost right away.

Getting used to Texas football was not quite as simple. T-Lloyd knew that he would have to improve. Many players in Texas are better than in New Orleans. The crowds for the games are also much bigger. The whole town of Hurst follows the "Blue Raiders."

When T-Lloyd met Bell's head coach, things got easier. Coach Gary Olivo saw something in T-Lloyd right away. He placed T-Lloyd on the junior varsity squad. By the end of the 2005 season, T-Lloyd was a starting offensive lineman. Coach Olivo was sure that T-Lloyd would be on the varsity next season. Things had happened quickly. This was less than six months since Hurricane *Katrina*.

The other members of the Blue Raiders liked T-Lloyd. They saw how hard he worked on every play. Being part of a football team is a very cool thing. Players are great friends on and off the field. Since they depend on each other so much, they become very close.

DeAnte Piper, a running back, is T-Lloyd's best friend on the team. "*All* the guys on the team are like family," T-Lloyd says. "They were down with me from day one. We're all tight." Laughing, he adds, "Everyone is always at my house. They love coming over for my mom's famous jambalaya. They've found out that the best food comes from New Orleans."

By the time T-Lloyd's sophomore year ended, he was enjoying his new life. He would always love New Orleans—but he was a Texan now. He was ready for bigger and better things on the football field.

T-Lloyd's Mom serves up some of her homemade jambalaya, which is a Louisiana Creole dish of Spanish and French creation.

Making friends has never been a problem for an outgoing guy like T-Lloyd. Here, he plays with his new iPhone while DeAnte watches a Brett Favre press conference on TV.

# CHAPTER FIVE

## NEW POSITION

T-Lloyd had a great summer in 2006. After everything that had happened, it was nice to relax. Of course, there was one thing he was really looking forward to: the start of football season. T-Lloyd wanted to make the varsity. He had been working hard to get ready. Also, Coach Olivo had given him some big news.

Coach wanted T-Lloyd to learn a new position. He talked to T-Lloyd about moving back to the *defensive* line. This is where T-Lloyd had played in middle school. Coach Olivo felt that nose tackle was the best position for T-Lloyd.

Football is an amazing game. On one hand, it's like a street fight. On the other hand, it's a battle of strategy. Coaches are always moving players and changing things around. It's all about finding a way to win. There are many kinds of offensive and defensive game plans.

Here's a good example: the "3-4" defense. This is a defense where three linemen play in front of four linebackers.

In the diagram above, the "X's" represent defensive players. The "O's" represent offensive players. The 3 "X's" directly across from the group of 6 "O's" are the defensive linemen. The "X" in the middle of those 3 "X's" is the nose tackle.

This makes it tougher for the offense to block the linebackers. The offense never knows which of them are going to rush. Most teams *can't* play a 3-4. That's because they need an extra lineman in the trenches. This helps to stop the other team's running game. The best way to make a 3-4 defense work is to have an awesome nose tackle.

Here's why: When the ball is snapped, the nose tackle must "eat up" the players blocking him. Eating up players means staying on them and keeping them busy. That way, they can't block other players. It's one of the toughest jobs in football. A nose tackle in the 3-4 usually has to eat up two or three players at a time. This lets the linebackers guard the pass *and* the run.

A good defense can be the difference between winning and losing. It comes down to what kind of players you have. With skilled linebackers and a huge lineman, a coach might play a 3-4. But most teams usually go with the 4-3. It has four linemen and three linebackers. This is the most balanced defense for guarding against the pass and the rush.

Strategy is what made Coach Olivo decide to move T-Lloyd to nose tackle. He wanted to start playing a 3-4 defense. First, he needed someone big and strong on the line. It would almost be like having an extra player. With T-Lloyd's skill, the coach knew it would work.

For T-Lloyd, it seemed perfect. He had always enjoyed playing defense. Plus, it might help him make it to the next level. Like many young football players, he dreams of playing in the NFL.

It's very hard to make it to the NFL. There are about 13,000 college seniors who are football players. The NFL draft has seven rounds. There are 32 teams in the league. This means that only about 250 players will get drafted.

Of course, the rewards are fantastic ... *if* you get there. In 2006, the New Orleans Saints drafted USC star running back Reggie Bush. He was the second pick in the draft. They signed him to a $54 million deal!

Every player in the NFL draft gets a pretty big contract. Marques Colston was the $252^{nd}$ pick in that same draft. That was only five picks away from not being drafted at all. Nobody even knew who he was. Still, he signed a deal for almost a million dollars. Not bad for a player who nearly went undrafted!

Here's the cool part, though. Most fans thought Reggie Bush was going to be a superstar. They didn't even worry about Marques Colston. But in the first game of the season, he was named as a starter. Playing wide receiver, he caught a touchdown pass! Colston went to on to have a great season. He almost won the Rookie of the Year award. His story shows that with hard work, it is possible to make it to the NFL.

Nobody knows this better than T-Lloyd. That's why he was so happy to switch to nose tackle. It was going be a tough challenge. But he would have a better chance of being an NFL draft pick. This is because nose tackle is a unique position. There are many quarterbacks, wide receivers, and linebackers. But only a few people can be good nose tackles.

T-Lloyd started his junior year ready to learn his new role. Luckily, he had a lot of help.

Defensive coordinator Andy Modica worked with T-Lloyd. He taught T-Lloyd things to make him a good nose tackle. T-Lloyd started practicing his new position. Coach Olivo felt that T-Lloyd was going to be a great nose tackle.

But T-Lloyd would have to prove how good he was. Practicing when the stands were empty was one thing. Playing a game in front of 8,000 fans would be much tougher. Yet, before the first game of the season, T-Lloyd wasn't nervous. He just wanted to get out there and play.

There's nothing like running onto the field before the first game of the year. The players wait for the announcer to give the signal. Then they come running out on the field. The fans cheer and take photos. This moment was special for T-Lloyd. There was nothing like playing in front of a big Texas crowd.

T-Lloyd's junior season went well. He did a good job in his new position. The new 3-4 defense worked well, too. The Blue Raiders became one of the best teams in the area.

By the last game of the season, T-Lloyd was already thinking about next year. It was going to be his senior year. He wanted to get even bigger and stronger. Nothing is more important for a nose tackle.

T-Lloyd knew what he needed to do. When the season ended, he got right to work.

# CHAPTER SIX

## PUMPING IRON

Once T-Lloyd became a nose tackle, everything changed. He had lifted weights before, but not all the time. To be good at his new position, he would need to get stronger.

Luckily, Bell had a nice gym. T-Lloyd was ready to get started. It was tough at first, though. He had to force himself to wake up early every day to get to the gym before school! Soon, however, he looked forward to his alarm clock ringing before the sun came up. After just a couple weeks of pumping iron, T-Lloyd was hooked.

The coaches were amazed by how strong T-Lloyd was getting. He went from big to *huge* in a short amount of time. Soon T-Lloyd was one of the strongest members of the team. He was able to match anyone on the bench press and the squat.

When it comes to size and strength, everyone is different. It's not just how hard you work in the weight room. Some people are naturally strong. T-Lloyd is one of those people. Still, it took a lot of time and effort to become huge.

That's exactly what Larry Allen did. Some people regard Allen as the strongest player in NFL history. Allen's hard work in the weight room made him different from other players. At 325 pounds, he was one of the best offensive linemen ever. In the weight room, he was even better. Most people try to bench a weight that is the same as what they weigh. Allen benched more than *double* his body weight—nearly 700 pounds!

Although T-Lloyd wasn't at that level, he was getting stronger and stronger. He enjoyed lifting weights almost as much as playing football. This is normal for football players. Most defensive and offensive linemen are into weightlifting.

For T-Lloyd, improvement is the key. The more weight you're able to lift, the stronger you're getting. Every couple of weeks he tries to add some extra weight. There's nothing better than putting another plate on the bar.

Weightlifting is not always easy, though. Sometimes you feel stuck. You can't lift bigger weights.

This happens to everybody. It's frustrating, that's for sure. It even happened to T-Lloyd.

**Even the strongest guys can get frustrated.**

One day, T-Lloyd was at the Bell High gym in a bad mood. He was tired, and he couldn't push through the set. There was only one other kid in the weight room. T-Lloyd had seen him around school. He had heard someone say that his name was ... wait, let's just make up a name. When you hear what he did, you'll understand why. So, let's just call him "Robbie."

Robbie saw that T-Lloyd was not able to push through his set. He stepped away from a squat machine and came up to T-Lloyd.

"What's up, T-Lloyd? You all right?" he asked.

"Yeah, man," T-Lloyd gave him a strange look.

He wasn't sure why this kid was talking to him. "I'm cool, thanks, just going through a rough time. Lately I haven't done well with my benching."

"I've been there," Robbie said. Then he took a few steps closer to T-Lloyd. He looked around the room to make sure nobody was around. "You need to do something to get stronger. How else you figure on playing college ball?" He reached into his backpack, "I got the pills you need."

Robbie was not a doctor. T-Lloyd knew exactly what "pills" he was talking about: steroids. T-Lloyd knew all about steroids. He had seen people on TV and on the Internet talking about it. Even his parents and coaches had warned him about steroids.

A lot of people don't even know what steroids are. Very simply, they are man-made male hormones. In your body, there already *are* male hormones. That's normal. But when you take steroids, the amount of male hormones in your body gets too high. That's dangerous and it is *not* normal.

Male hormones help a boy's body develop. They grow muscles, and hair on their bodies. You don't want to mess with how many hormones are in your body by taking steroids. If you do, crazy things might happen. For example, taking steroids can make your testicles get smaller. They can make you go bald. They can even cause you to develop breasts. What guy wants *any* of those things?

Steroids can be taken as pills, liquid, or cream.

They can also be taken as a shot. Steroids are not new. In fact, they've been around for more than 100 years.

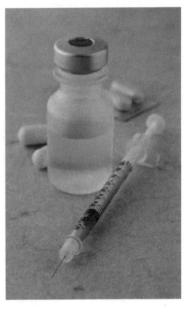

During the 1950s, many weightlifters found out about steroids. They learned that steroids can help you grow bigger and stronger. Athletes around the world started using them to get ready for the Olympics. They didn't worry about the bad things steroids can do to your body. Finally, steroids were not allowed anymore in the Olympics. They are now also illegal in every major sport.

Of course, that hasn't stopped some pro athletes from using them. This was talked about in the "Mitchell Report." In 2007, Senator George Mitchell was hired by Major League Baseball.

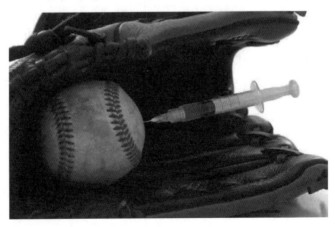

They wanted Senator Mitchell to see how many pro baseball players were using steroids. What he found out surprised people. The Senator said that 80 baseball players had taken them. He also said that they were not the only ones. He felt that many more Major Leaguers had also taken steroids.

Through the years, some high school athletes have taken steroids. Why? They want to build up muscle quickly. That way, they can be better football, baseball, or basketball players. They've heard that some college and pro athletes do it. But, as T-Lloyd knows, it's *very* dangerous. Plus, if you are ever caught, you can forget about a college scholarship.

"What do you think?" Robbie looked at T-Lloyd with a smile. He showed T-Lloyd the bottle of pills in his hand. "I can give you the first pill free—just to try it out." To Robbie's surprise, T-Lloyd shook his head.

"You need to get that stuff away from me, man. Or else you and me will have a problem." Then T-Lloyd stood up. He gave Robbie the same tough look he gave to other linemen. "Right now," T-Lloyd said.

"Okay, man, take it easy." Robbie put the pills back in his bag. He quickly walked away with a scared look on his face.

T-Lloyd got back to his workout. He pushed through his final set.

Luckily for Robbie, Lyle Alzado wasn't there at that moment. He also would have told Robbie to get lost. Alzado was an NFL star in the 1970s and 1980s. He was also a steroids user. He admitted it after his career was over. Sadly, Alzado died from a brain tumor at age 43. Many people believe his death was because of taking steroids.

**If you use steroids, you are risking everything . Is it worth it?**

There will always be people who try to cheat. Some will cheat on tests instead of studying. Others will steal money instead of getting a job and earning it. In sports, some athletes will take steroids. They are just cheating.

Everyone knows what happens when you do something wrong. If you cheat on a test, you'll be given an "F." If you get caught stealing, you can go to jail. And if you use steroids, you can die. That's what Lyle Alzado would have told Robbie.

Pro sports are trying to keep drugs out of their leagues. There's nothing more exciting than sports.

No athlete should cheat *and* risk his life.

T-Lloyd lifted weights for the rest of the school year, and then the summer. He felt better than ever before. He was going to be a senior. That meant that college wasn't far off. This was important to him. He knew that he would need to have a great season next year. That was the only way he could earn a college scholarship.

T-Lloyd's parents had always taught him two things. One was the love of football. The other was how important it is to go to college. They had worked hard their whole lives. All they wanted was to give their sons the chance to go to college.

But Hurricane *Katrina* had come along and destroyed their home. After that, money was tight. Paying for college would be difficult for Mr. and Mrs. Lloyd. T-Lloyd wanted to earn a college scholarship. It would be the greatest gift he could ever give to his parents—and to himself.

# CHAPTER SEVEN

## BIG GAME

"You guys know how important this game is," Coach Olivo said. He looked right at his players. "Go out there and play hard. Win the game for your friends and your family. Win it for Bell!"

The players put on their helmets and ran out of the locker room. T-Lloyd was ready. This game meant a lot. This was a chance for Bell to get to the playoffs. Then maybe they could win the state title. The Blue Raiders ran onto the field. As they did, the big crowd started cheering.

This was a big game. The Blue Raiders were facing a tough team. They were called the South Grand

Prairie "Warriors." The year before, the Warriors had beaten the Blue Raiders 35-6. T-Lloyd would never forget that game. He had hurt his ankle on the *very first play* of the game. His ankle had blown up to the size of a grapefruit. T-Lloyd wasn't able to play the rest of that game. Today was going to be payback time ... hopefully.

Both teams were playing hard as they could. After three quarters, the Warriors led 14-8. T-Lloyd and his teammates were playing a good game. But the Warriors were playing great defense. As hard as Bell tried, they couldn't score many times.

In the fourth quarter, T-Lloyd was at his best. The Warriors couldn't get past him. They were throwing two offensive linemen at him. But T-Lloyd was working hard. He didn't want to let the Warriors score any more points.

The problem was that Bell still couldn't score. Seconds kept ticking off the clock. Soon there were only two minutes left in the game! Things weren't looking too good for Bell. Then they got even worse. The Warriors made it down to Bell's 30-yard line. They had the ball and the lead, with the clock ticking away. A few yards closer and they would be able to kick a field goal. That would put them up by 9. If that happened, Bell would lose for sure. T-Lloyd and his team-mates simply could not allow the Warriors to score.

**T-Lloyd couldn't help but stare at the yellow uprights. After all, a field goal would pretty much end the game.**

On first down, the ball was snapped. The center placed his hands on the "72" on T-Lloyd's jersey. He gave T-Lloyd a hard push. At first, that made T-Lloyd lose his balance. But he got back on his feet. He looked at Daniel Pressman, the Warriors' quarterback. Pressman was dropping back to throw the ball. T-Lloyd put his left arm into the air just in time. He got his hand on Pressman's pass. The ball fell to the ground, stopping the clock. The Bell crowd jumped to its feet and cheered.

On second down, T-Lloyd was sure it was going to be a run. He was right. Pressman handed the ball off to the running back.

The center and another offensive lineman were both trying to knock T-Lloyd down. One of them struck him in the ribs. The other one tried to knock him down with a blow to his chest. But T-Lloyd wouldn't back down. He hit right back, knocking *both* guys off-balance. Then, with one free arm, he reached out. He was trying to make a tackle on the running back. T-Lloyd grabbed his ankle and held on tight. This slowed the running back down for a moment.

That's all it took. One of T-Lloyd's teammates ran over. He tackled the running back. It was a gain of only one yard! T-Lloyd had done his job again. "Playing nose guard is not about stats," he says. "It's about *football*. It's about lining up across from the biggest guys on the field. It's about banging heads, and seeing who the real men are."

Now, it was third and nine. Everybody knew that a pass was coming. Coach Olivo called the defensive play from the sideline. The Bell middle linebackers were named Taniela Vake and K.C. Aharanawa. Both of them would blitz right up the middle. In the huddle, Taniela looked right at T-Lloyd. He said, "It's on you. You gotta hold up those two inside guys!"

**The Bell defensive line prepares for the biggest play of the game.**

T-Lloyd nodded. He understood what Taniela was saying. It was up to *him* to fight against two blockers. That would leave only one blocker to take on Taniela and K.C. If T-Lloyd did his job, one of them would have a chance to get to the quarterback. They had to sack him before he passed the ball for a first down.

By now, the fans were on their feet. They were cheering loudly. Everybody knew how important this play was. The Warriors had the ball and a six-point lead. If they scored, the game was over. But if Bell could stop them, they would have one last chance. Then Bell could get the ball back and try to score a touchdown for the win.

When the ball was hiked, T-Lloyd slammed into the two blockers on the line. This wasn't going to be easy, because they were *huge*. The center put his hands into T-Lloyd's chest. Then the offensive guard attacked T-Lloyd also. They tried to stop T-Lloyd, but he would not go down.

The three players kept on fighting each other. T-Lloyd was tired after a long and hard game. Still, he didn't give up. He charged back into them using all his strength. One player fell to the ground. The other player fought back, but T-Lloyd overpowered him.

Meanwhile, Taniela and K.C. had a chance. Because T-Lloyd was keeping that lineman busy, there was a hole in the line. Taniela ran right through it and crashed into Daniel Pressman. He sacked him for a ten-yard loss! The Warriors were too far away to even try a field goal. They would have to punt. T-Lloyd and his teammates had stopped them cold! Bell called their final timeout. They were ready to get the ball back with a final chance to win.

As T-Lloyd ran off the field, he was very tired. He was so beaten up that he could barely move. That's how tough it is to play in the trenches. He picked up a water bottle and splashed cool water on his face.

The crowd was excited and so were the players. Everybody knew that Bell still had a chance to win. That was thanks to T-Lloyd and the defensive line. Now it was up to the offense. The Blue Raiders made it down the field. Soon they were on the Warriors' 20-yard line. But there were only 15 seconds left to play.

Over on the sideline, T-Lloyd was cheering for his teammates. That's what football is all about. "We're brothers," T-Lloyd says. "Sure, we did our job on the defensive end, but that doesn't matter. We win or lose as a team."

It was third down and one. But a first down wouldn't help the Blue Raiders now. That's because there was so little time left on the clock. It was time to go for it all. Quarterback Logan Smith dropped back to pass. He looked for someone to throw to. Then Logan saw one of his receivers, Atem Bol. He saw that Atem was running straight to the end zone. Logan threw the ball. It was a little high, but Atem jumped up and made a great catch in the end zone. Touchdown, Bell!

The noise was *very* loud. T-Lloyd, his teammates, and the huge crowd were cheering. The extra point was good a moment later. It had been a great comeback. Bell had won, 15-14. They were going to the playoffs!

For T-Lloyd, this was big. As a senior, there was no next year for him at Bell. His time was *now*. It had been a tough high school career. He had lived through Hurricane *Katrina*. But that had been just the beginning. He had to move to a different state, make new friends and start on a new team. But T-Lloyd had done it, and now it was paying off.

In the locker room, reporters were talking to Logan Smith and Atem Bol. They wanted to know all about that touchdown pass. As usual, the defensive linemen were not asked many questions.

All of a sudden, the Warriors' coach walked in the locker room. First he shook hands with Coach Olivo. Then he walked over to T-Lloyd's locker and held out his hand. "That was a heck of a game you played, son. You were the toughest guy in the trenches today. I can't remember the last time I've seen a lineman as good as you were today."

Guys who play on the line live for moments like these. They understand that most people don't really think about them too much. Most people just think about positions like quarterback or running back.

That's why T-Lloyd was so happy. To have a coach say something like that after the game is very cool.

T-Lloyd's high school career was almost over. But he knew he was playing the game the right way. Games like this proved it. All that hard work was paying off. T-Lloyd felt that he could take the next step. He was getting ready for college. It would be just one more challenge in a lifetime of challenges.

Chillin' in the pool: T-Lloyd's positive attitude continues to help him overcome obstacles and achieve great things on the football field, socially, and in the classroom.

# CHAPTER EIGHT

## T-LLOYD

Thomas Lloyd III—T-Lloyd—has a lot to be proud about. He has faced a lot of tough things in his life. He had to deal with Hurricane *Katrina*. That's more than most kids ever go through. Because of it, his family had to move to a new state. T-Lloyd had to change schools right before his sophomore year of high school. He also had to start all over again as a football player on a new team.

T-Lloyd could have quit on his dreams. Instead, he became stronger. He is planning for a great future. Of course, he dreams of starring in the NFL. But he knows that most NFL linemen don't play very long. A normal career for a lineman is about four seasons. That's because of all the pounding they take.

So it hasn't been only football for T-Lloyd. Sure, he's been busy with practice, games, and lifting weights. Still, he has kept up his grades. He has become an honors student at Bell, with a 3.2 grade-point average.

During his high school career, T-Lloyd showed how good he is on the football field. Along with fine grades, there was no doubt he would be going to college. As a matter of fact, many colleges got in touch with him. Some of them offered him a full scholarship. T-Lloyd was on his way. He is going to be the first member of his family to graduate college!

T-Lloyd is a great example of someone who didn't just play sports. He never forgot about his homework. "There are times that I'm tired from football or lifting weights," he says. "But I have a long life ahead of me, whether or not I make the NFL. I want a good career after my playing days are over. College is my ticket to that career."

T-Lloyd wants to study business or marketing in college. A college degree will make him important to any company. He is also a friendly and nice guy. That helps when you're out in the business world.

If you're a college football fan, there's an important date each year. It comes on the first Wednesday in February. That day is known as "National Signing Day." It's for high school football players. This is when they sign a letter to go to whatever college they choose.

T-Lloyd the businessman.

In 2008, National Signing Day fell on Wednesday, February 6. That was the proudest day of T-Lloyd's life. Of course, he had a tough decision to make. He had three fantastic schools to choose from: Fordham University, Abilene Christian University, and the Virginia Military Institute. They had each offered him a full scholarship.

These great colleges all have good business classes. So no matter where T-Lloyd went, he couldn't lose. Those colleges are also good football schools. That's what made the decision hard. T-Lloyd has big dreams on the football field. He needed to choose a college team that would help him improve in football.

It was early in the morning on Wednesday, February 6, 2008. All of a sudden, there was a lot of cheering and happy screams. T-Lloyd had just told his family his decision. He had decided to attend Fordham University. His mother cried in happiness. She wouldn't stop hugging her giant son.

Fordham is a small private school located in New York City. It's a long way from Hurst, Texas. That's okay with T-Lloyd. College is all about new adventures. He has never lived anywhere besides Texas or New Orleans. Going to New York City will be a dream come true. Yes, it's gong to be hard to be so far away from his family. But T-Lloyd is ready for the next part of his life.

**A building at Fordham University.**

Fordham is a smaller school than many other colleges. Still, it's a great football college. It's a perfect place for T-Lloyd to play and improve. Remember, he's only been playing nose tackle for a couple of years. He will get good coaching and college experience. Who can imagine how good he will be after a couple more years?

Many players from Fordham have gone on to play in the NFL. The most famous of them was a coach. He was even talked about in the first chapter of this book: Vince Lombardi. He went to Fordham in the 1930s.

Lombardi would later go on to coach the Green Bay Packers. He turned them into champions. The Packers had been a pretty bad team until he became the coach. Then he led them to *five* NFL championships. After Coach Lombardi retired, he was given a big honor. Each year, the team that wins the Super Bowl is awarded a trophy. It's what every NFL team plays for. The trophy is now called the *Vince Lombardi* Trophy.

T-Lloyd hopes that one day he will go on to the NFL also. However, his dreams don't end there. His interest in weightlifting became even more serious. T-Lloyd decided to take it to the next level. He joined the Bell power lifting squad. He also began competing around Texas. By his senior year, he was ranked in the top 10 in his area. He has squatted 550 pounds and bench-pressed 360 pounds!

T-Lloyd would like to take weightlifting to the highest level in the world: the Olympics.

There is no football competition in the Olympics. Of course, there is for weightlifting. It's good that he stayed clean and didn't take steroids.

T-Lloyd may or may not end up at the Olympics, or in the NFL. No matter what, he is going to be a big success in life. His love of football was the starting point. Since then, it has been all about determination and hard work.

It makes a lot of sense that T-Lloyd is a nose tackle. In many ways, it fits who he is. He's the one in the trenches doing his job to help his team win. That's what he's all about.

T-Lloyd has been in New Orleans and Texas. Now he's on his way to Fordham University. All of them will be better places because T-Lloyd was there. He's a huge kid with an even bigger heart. T-Lloyd always seems to have a smile on his face. So if you ever see him walking down the street, be sure to say hello. He was born Thomas Lloyd III. His family calls him T.J. But to everybody else—his teammates, classmates, and friends—he's just T-Lloyd.

In the trenches, it's all about heart.
How big is yours?